SWEAR WORD

Go to Hell, Bitch!

Vol. 2

Mandala Adult Coloring Book
Patterns For Relaxation And Stress Relief

COLOR TEST PAGE

COLOR TEST PAGE

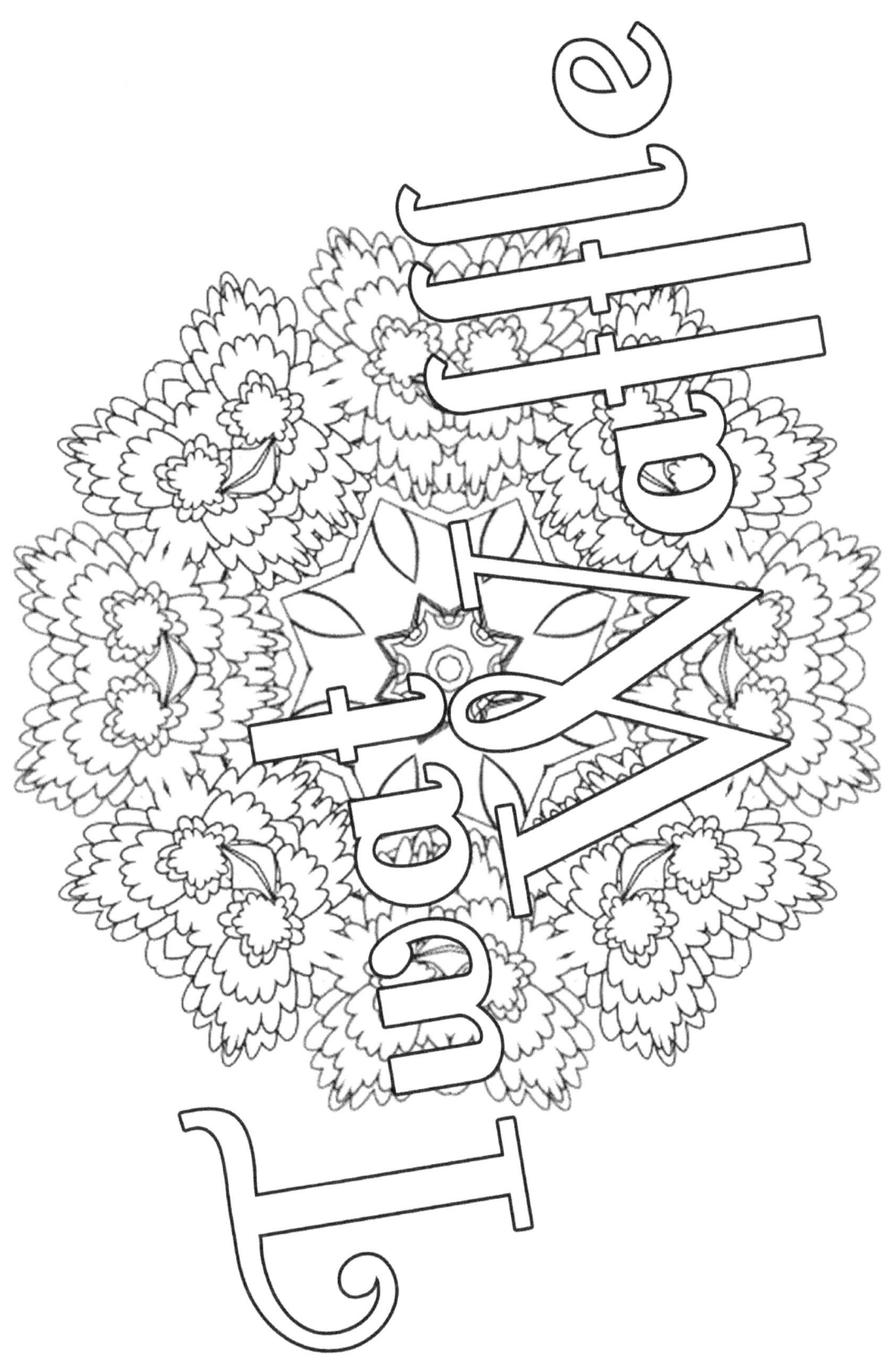

www.ingramcontent.com/pod-product-compliance
Lightning Source LLC
Chambersburg PA
CBHW080554190526
45169CB00007B/2772